I am Going to the Hospital to Have Surgery

a story by,

How to use this story?

Read the story prior to the event or activity. Read it several times a day or during the week so the child learns what to expect and what the expected behavior is. Use the visuals on the last page to remind the child of the sequence during the activity or event. If the child is successful read the celebratory story to celebrate and positively reinforce the child's behavior.

I need to go to the hospital to have surgery.

I will put on hospital pajamas called a gown.

I will lay in a hospital bed.

The nurse will put an IV in my hand.

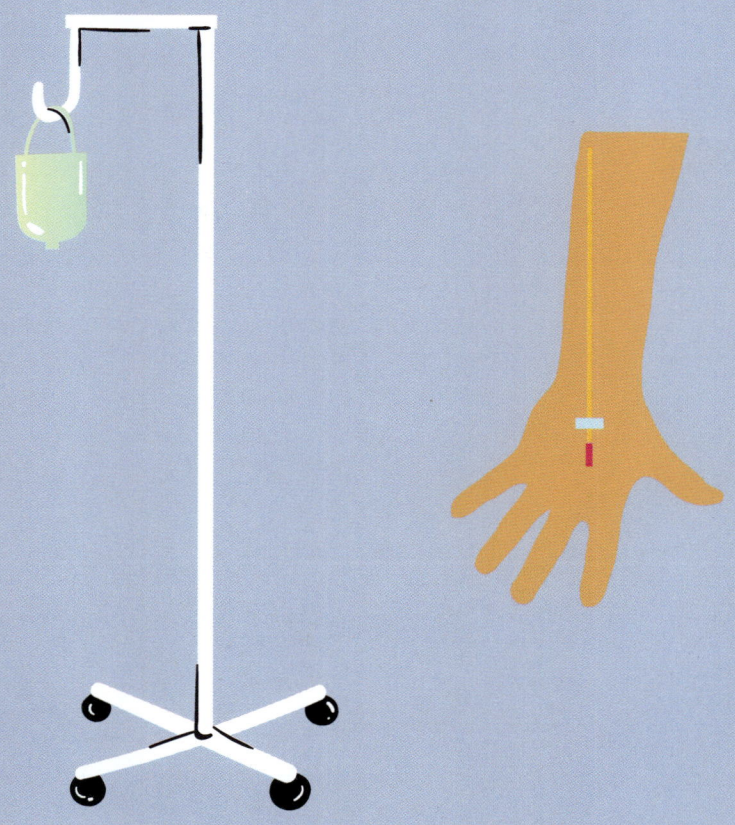

An IV is used to get medicine in my body.

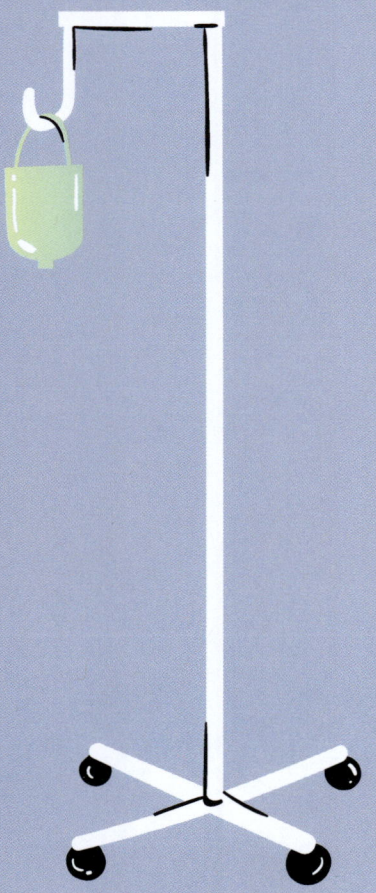

I need to keep the tube in my hand so the medicine can get in my body.

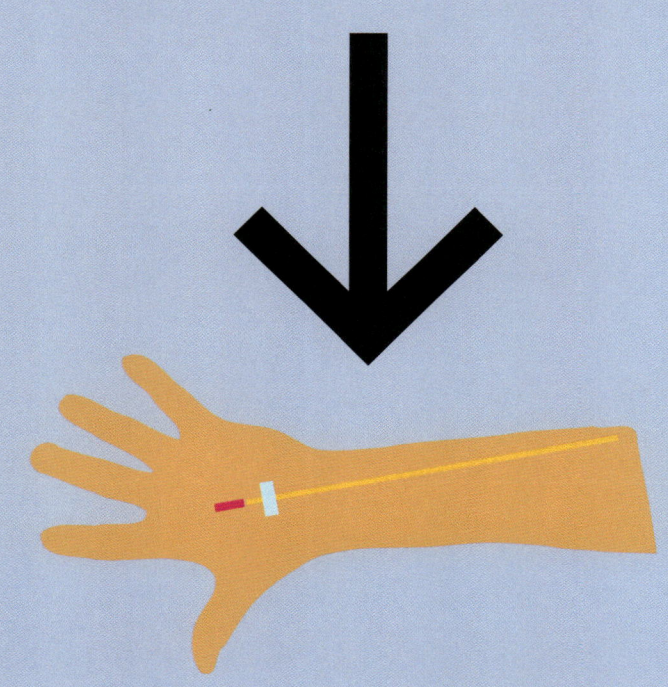

When I keep the IV in my hand it makes my doctor, nurse, mom, and dad happy.

The medicine helps me feel no pain

I will try and keep the IV in my hand.
I will be very brave

The nurse or doctor will put medicine in my IV so I can sleep during my surgery.

After surgery I will wake up and might feel really tired and sore.

My cyst will be gone

After surgery I might have a stomach ache and feel like I need to throw up

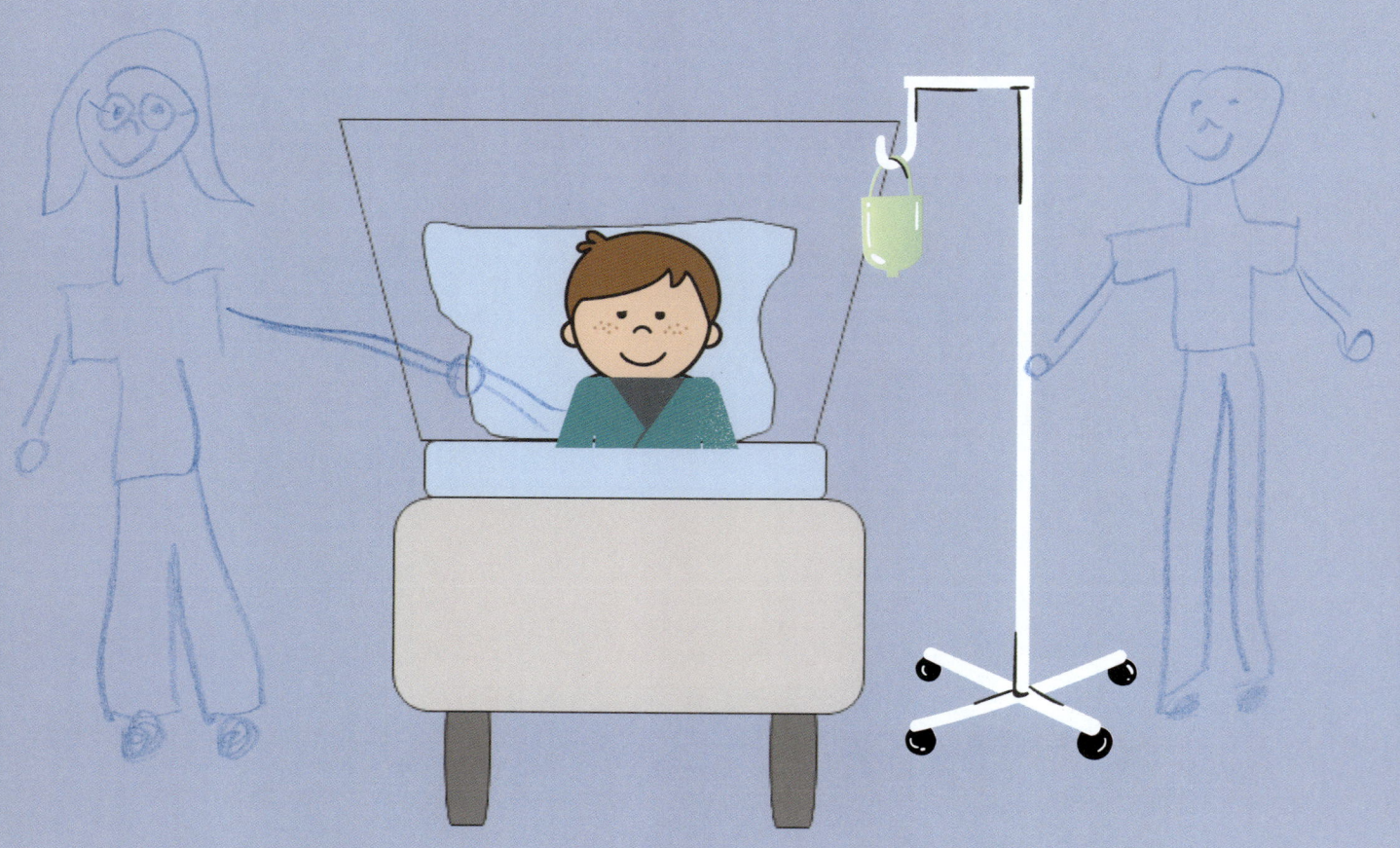

The nurse can give me medicine in my IV to help my tummy feel better after surgery.

When I am awake and feeling better I can go home.

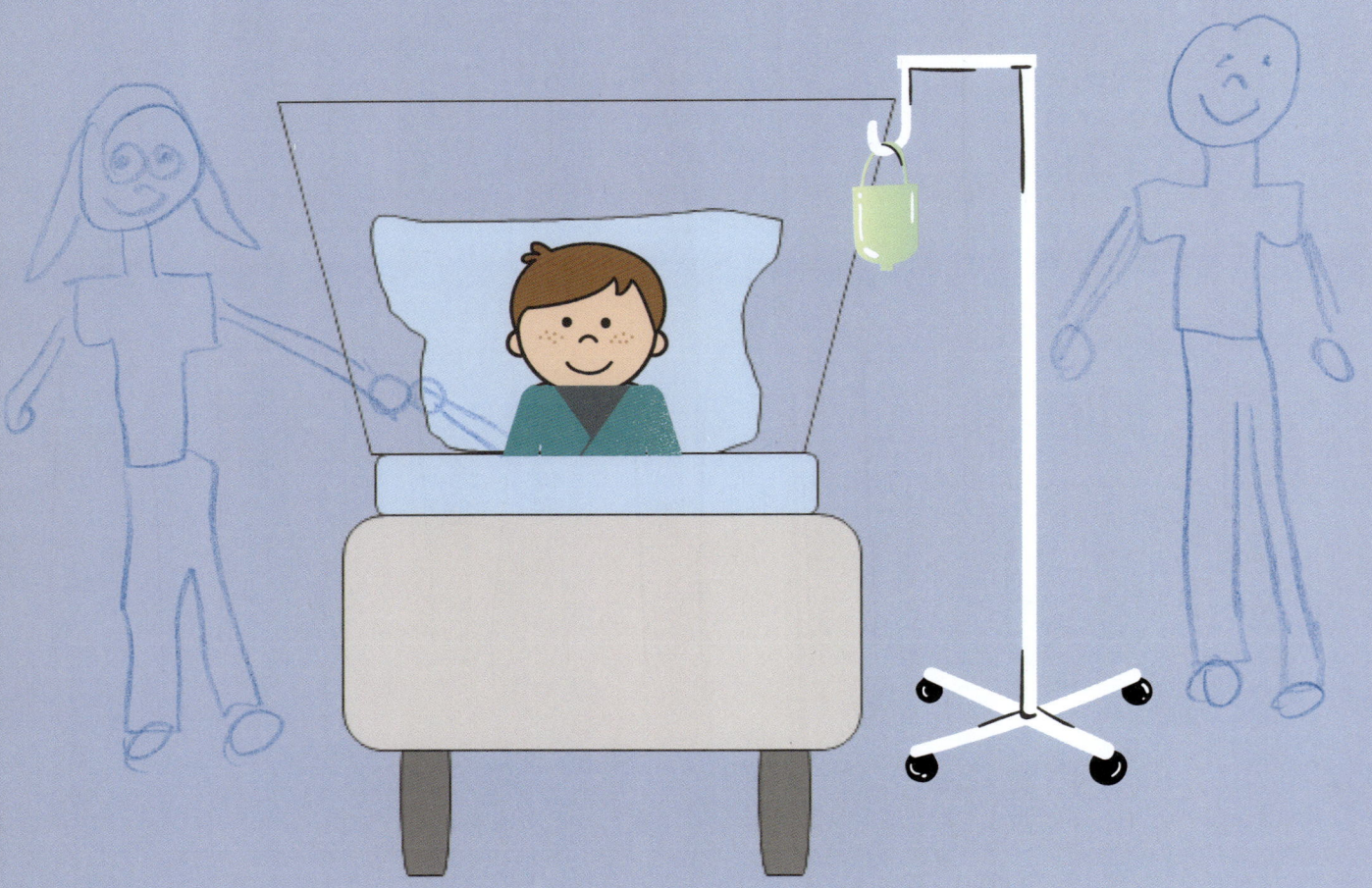

I put on my clothes.

I am ready to go home.

Use these pictures during the day of the surgery.

1. Put on gown.

2. Lay in bed.

3. Get IV.
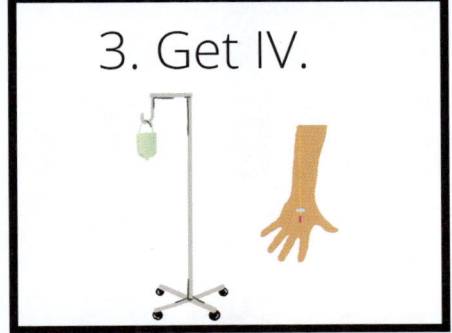

4. Go to sleep.

5. Wake up.

6. Get dressed and go home.

Read the celebration story next to reinforce the behavior.

I Did a Good Job at the Hospital

I did a good job at the hospital.

I put on a gown and laid in my hospital bed.

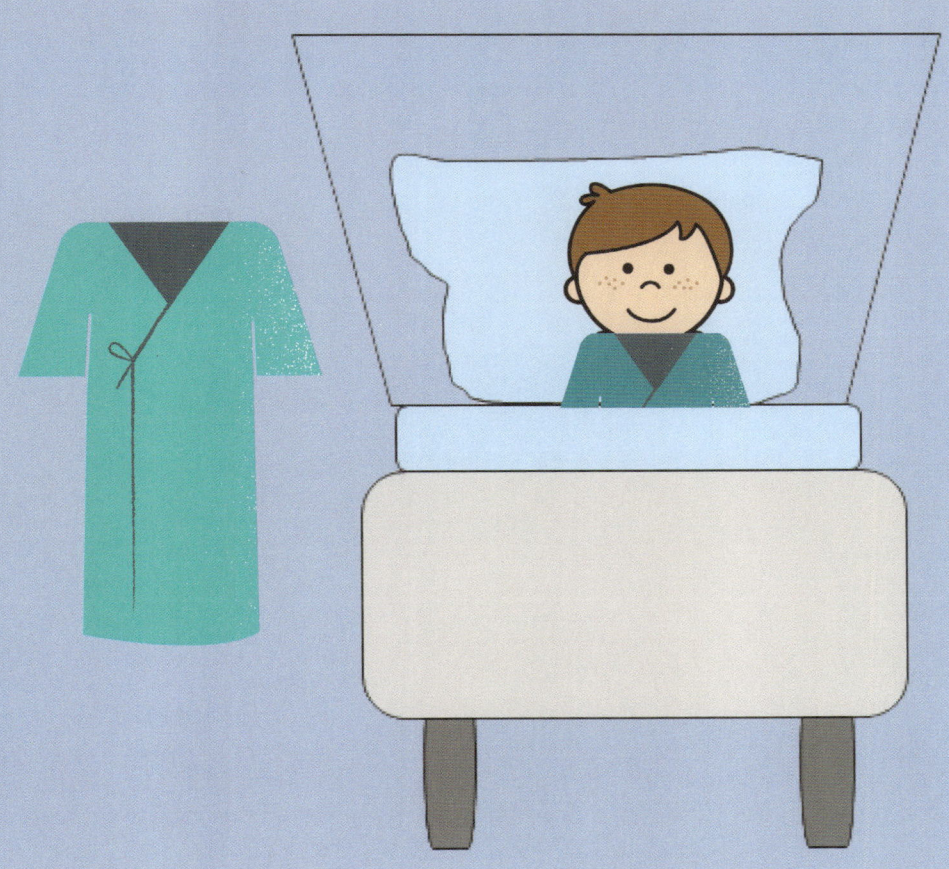

I used quiet hands and kept my IV in my hand.

I went to sleep.

I waited until the doctor said I could go home.

I made my mom, dad, nurse, and doctor happy.

To learn more about Positively Prepared and other stories they offer please visit the website at
www.positivelypreparedstories.com

About the Author

Heather McKay is a Speech and Language Pathologist who works with children in the school setting and is also a survivor of childhood cancer. She understands the anxiety that children and parents go through when going through a medical procedure or treatment. She has witnessed firsthand when working with her students how powerful these stories are at accomplishing a desired positive behavior. Using her childhood cancer experience and professional skills of writing social narratives, she created Positively Prepared stories.

Printed in Great Britain
by Amazon